*to Mam & Dad*

# The Seer Sung Husband

Bob Beagrie

Published 2010 by
Smokestack Books
PO Box 408, Middlesbrough TS5 6WA
e-mail : info@smokestack-books.co.uk
www.smokestack-books.co.uk

**The Seer Sung Husband**
Bob Beagrie
Cover image: Peter Hesleton
Cover photo: Kevin Howard
Inner Images: Andy Broderick

Printed by
EPW Print & Design Ltd

ISBN 978-0-9560341-4-4
Smokestack Books gratefully
acknowledges the support of
Arts Council England

**LOTTERY FUNDED**

Smokestack Books is
represented by Inpress Ltd
www.inpressbooks.co.uk

The youth, returning to his mistress, hies,
And impudent in hope, with ardent eyes,
And beating breast, by the dear statue lies.'

Ovid, *Metamorphoses*

'As now she might have done,
So much to my good comfort, as it is
Now piercing my soul. O thus she stood,
Even with such life of majesty, warm life,
As now it coldly stands, when first I woo'd her!
I am ashamed: does not the stone rebuke me
For being more stone than it? O royal piece,
There's magic in thy majesty...'

Leontes in *The Winter's Tale*

# Foreword

It is high time to publish the manuscript that has accompanied me across so much time and space, kept safe in a box in a locked case, in cellars and in attics of the homes I have lived in. Often forgotten for years as the world transformed, then suddenly remembered on the first appearance of a new idea, a new invention that she predicted or news of a fresh atrocity she foresaw. For many years the manuscript, along with other valuable documents, was lost, stolen by a traitor of The Brethren and sold to one Richard Head, who used the records for his own profit and in 1667 published a book of Ursula's prophecies, which he later admitted to having wholly fabricated. Since then other writers and editors have invented, embellished and added their versions of her predictions to the palimpsest of rumour, legend, folklore and hearsay, including Samuel Pepys, George Coleman and Boz himself, until she has now all but vanished, save as a caricature, a puppet, a pantomime dame kept alive for the sake of tourism.

When the original scribbled manuscript was finally returned to me I discovered some pages damaged by fire, water and mildew, while one or two crucial entries remained missing. I confess to rewriting these as best I could from memory. In the process of preparing the whole document for publication I have reworked the entire original diary to make it more comprehensible to the contemporary reader, and have, after long contemplation, altered some sections and abridged others, particularly in the light of certain historical developments. However I hope to have retained much of the authenticity, and indeed the truth of the events of which I speak, and by doing so make a belated response to Mr Dudley Costello's comments in his article printed in *Household Words*, August 1856 in which he speculates "*His fame rests entirely on the fact of his having bestowed his name on the bewitching Ursula; for, with that exception, we hear nothing of him at all... Toby Shipton either crawled through life the most hen pecked of husbands, or shuffled off his mortal coil after a brief season of conjugal felicity.*" It is my intention that this publication demonstrates that neither is the case.

**Mr T. Shipton, The Seer Sung Husband**

# Dramatis Personae

### Old Mother Shipton (1488-1561)
Legendary English soothsayer and witch, born Ursula
Sontheil in a cave in Knaresborough near Harrogate, North
Yorkshire. She is reported to have exhibited prophetic and
psychic abilities from an early age. At 24, she married Toby
Shipton and eventually became known as Mother Shipton.

### Henry VIII (1491-1547)
King of England and Lord of Ireland. Later King of Ireland
and claimant to the Kingdom of France. Henry was the
second monarch of the House of Tudor, succeeding his
father, Henry VII. Henry VIII was a significant figure in the
history of the English monarchy. He brought about the
English Reformation, which included the creation of the
Church of England, the Dissolution of the Monasteries, and
establishing the English monarch as the Supreme Head of the
Church of England.

### Cardinal Thomas Wolsey (c1473-1530)
English statesman and a cardinal of the Roman Catholic
Church. When Henry VIII became king in 1509, Wolsey's
affairs prospered and he soon became the controlling figure
in all matters of state. The highest position he attained was
Lord Chancellor in 1515. Wolsey's unpopularity amongst the
English nobility and his eventual failure to secure a divorce
for King Henry from his first wife Catherine of Aragon led to
his downfall. He was arrested for high treason in Yorkshire
and died at St. Mary's Abbey, Leicester on his journey to
London to face trial.

### Thomas Cromwell, 1st Earl of Essex (c1485-1540)
English statesman who served as King Henry VIII's chief
minister from 1532 to 1540. Cromwell was the most
prominent of those who suggested to Henry VIII that the
king make himself head of the English Church, and saw the
Act of Supremacy of 1534 through Parliament. As Henry
VIII's vicar-general, he presided over the Dissolution of the
Monasteries.

**Thomas Howard, 3rd Duke of Norfolk** (1473-1554)
A prominent Tudor politician. Uncle of Anne Boleyn and Godfather to Prince Edward. While remaining a Catholic he conducted the campaign against the Pilgrimage of Grace in 1537.

**Robert Aske** (1500-1537)
English attorney from a gentry family in Yorkshire, who became the leader of the insurgents in Northern rebellions known as The Pilgrimage of Grace in 1536. A moderate leader who encouraged his followers to trust the King's guarantee of safe conduct. Following further outbreaks of insurrection Aske was arrested, tried in London and executed in York for treason in July 1537.

**Robert Esch**
Friar of Knaresborough. Bill poster and propagandist for The Pilgrimage of Grace.

**John ap Rice**
One of Thomas Cromwell's commissioners in the preliminaries to the Dissolution of the Monasteries and interrogator of certain suspects involved in the Pilgrimage of Grace.

# Part 1
# MDXII

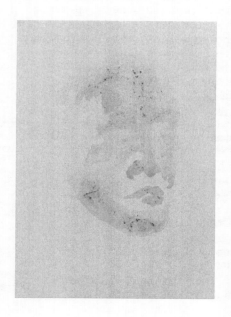

*'As the holly grows green*
*And never changes hue,*
*So I am - ever have been -*
*unto my lady true.'*

Henry VIII, *Green Grows the Holly*

.

The snow is melting on the eves.
There, the sound of its slide on tiles,
the muffled slump as it hits the midden,
then quiet returns to this moonless night.
My ears are pricked for I cannot sleep,
nor move with intent a clay-like muscle
as if our bed were the Dropping Well
that will turn flesh, bone or cloth to stone.
I'll likely lie here still in pale dawn's light,
chasing thoughts about the room,
in and out of shadows, through spider webs
and pest holes in the timbers, and this
on my wedding night, with my bride
sound asleep beside me snoring. The witch.

I wonder how this came to pass and only
in these witching hours share the worries
of my closest friends, my family; indeed
the whole of Knaresborough speculates
on how Ursula ensnared me - 'Toby,
that strapping lad with prospects,
who's shone in the gaze of many a girl?'
And in the morning will I wake and recall
nothing of these misgivings, shrugging off
the warnings like a mud-soiled shawl?

I shall take my saw, my chisels, my plane
and lose my night-fears amongst the grain,
the oak dust and shavings of the grand cabinet;
standing in my workshop, all but finished
ready for varnish. A fine thing, unblemished,
perfect in form, fit for a lady's private chambers,
fit for an Abbot or our brave new King.

My sleeping love, my Galatea shifts
and rocks beside me, her gentle breath stirs
the room, this house, the street and quiet vale,
her profile blemished as a twisted yew,
though the grain is good, I trust. Besides,
beauty of the outer bark is oft suspect
when the core and heartwood warp within.
Not so my deformed bride, whose eyes shine
with crystal truths set in a bed of cavern rock.
But how she suffers such capricious dreams
and reads secrets in the flight of birds,
tomorrow's patterns in the splash of trout,
this freeman's fate in a coil of smoke;
who'll answer before my tongue can speak.


'Hag Face,' some still dare call her
behind her back, 'Offspring of a harlot
and the Devil himself, born in a cave
in a thunder storm on the wrong side o' the Nidd',
to which, she replies, her expression stony,
*My Dear, we all of us live in the cave all our lives*
*and few peer out of its dim sympathies.*
But those in power are prone to burn or drown
or prick such folk that see with the second sight,
and claim that biblical right from the papal bull
of Innocent III and Exodus, though my bride
seems unconcerned by mistaken Maleficia.
Her infamy spreads along strands of gossip
through the lanes and dales of Yorkshire.

How many husbands, between two sips of ale
call their wives a witch, off hand, and wiping
white froth from the lip, suspect some pact
and fear malochia? But how many return
to hearth to hear the future pour in nightly babble
straight from her sleeping mouth, while lying
elf-addled beside her? My guess is fewer.

It begins a low drone, like insects in a hive,
to a guttural moan, a long sniff, hiss, a gulp,
as if she's bitten off of piece of night - that is
nothing more than a crust of what will come,
steeped in its taste as it's boiled in its juice,
it gathers like bile upon the breath, she balks
a trickle that spurts into a torrential flood.

*Three sleeping mountains gather breath*
*and spew out mud, and ice and death.*
*Earthquakes swallow town and drown*
*lands as yet to me unknown.*

Her eyelids flicker, clamp tight as knots,
the balls beneath them roll, sweat spots
pepper her knuckled brow, and I feel an urge
to plug the broken dam, to stop the surge
before I'm washed away and drowned
in unchecked seer song. She vomits isles
that rise from the ocean bed, a dragon's tail
that cracks the sky, silver serpents that feed
on fire, slither up the chimney chute;
on the hearthstone a salamander squirms
like a man accused of heresy, rooks cascade
against the shutters, a dairy maid kicks a pebble
across World's End Bridge, the bed I made
sails a lake of sloe gin, banewort, fungal fantasie.

Until the geyser of her mumblings cease,
the eddies run away and she soundly sleeps
once more, like a fallen log of elm
on a bed of soil under a coverlet of ivy.
And still I lie, listening to the frost dislodge
and slide across the slates, filled with love
for her crude, uncanny figure. Little by little
I am becoming accustomed to the searing dark -
as used to it as anyone can, who does not see
beneath the peel of one moment's fruit
without splitting the rind and tasting the pulp;
but feels the spirits in the air, the imps'
mischievous play like the charge before
a storm and who hears them as she speaks.


That time, I took the Long Walk when the gales
had passed, the Nidd full to bursting, rain still
falling on soaking mulch and the space alive
with energies. I was tired of the taverns,
the company of grumbling men, speculating
on the King and his brother's widow, his uneasy
peace with France, the Church's hidebound stance;
wearied by the false affections of frivolous women.
Beside the path near the Dropping Well she lay,
a frog on her shoulder, Hen of The Woods
growing from her thigh. A hum in the air like a
thousand angry bees, I stooped to brush away
the leaf litter of gold and copper and beheld
the form within the form a true carpenter perceives.
The moment his eyes settle on timber, it speaks.

In the evenings local people often pay a visit
from the village, the surrounding farms, from York.
Those with questions like hot chestnuts scorching
their minds and coins burning holes in purses.
She has me close the shutters, light the tallow,
stoke the fire and toss a sprig of dried lavender
into the flames. I set a bowl of water on the table,
between a vial of ink and a small athame.
I settle her on the chair in the farthest corner,
wrap a robe about her shoulders, then a shawl,
and tie a black scarf neatly about her head.
And as the shadows play, the heavy smoke coils,
it seems she watches my preparations
with the patience of a barn owl in a cemetery.


They pay a shilling in the antechamber,
knock three times and enter, bidding Ursula
by the fire good health. She listens to their tales
of woe, their yarns of hate, mundane worries.
I stand hidden by the screen and listen too,
as secrets fill the half-filled bowl. *Mistress,*
*where lies my stolen coat? How to find my fortune?*
*A charm needed to lift a hex from a cow.*
*How best to resurrect a long dead cock?*
*Shall I walk to the thirteenth field*
*in a red dress under a new moon and pick*
*wild flowers there to lay under his pillow?*
*Is the boy who calls me Father the true seed*
*of my loins? Will my wife bear me a son?*

They uncork the vial to tip a single drop
of ink into the scrying bowl: it clings, falls.
After the soft plop they slice a fingertip
with the blade and squeeze out a crimson drop,
then watch the threads of destiny swirl
in patterns of problems; affirmation, negation.
In the chamber's smoky atmosphere
they hunch over their own interpretation
squinting against the dancing light and peer
through circles of rippling reflection
at adulterer's swirls, strands of cuckold's pleas.
In the water slow illuminations appear
spiraling symbols, pictures, portraits,
writings that end with a signature, *Beag*.


You would think the lie would lash me
like a fishwife's tongue, ache like a knot
in my lower back, but you judge me harshly,
for she is as real as you or I, no simple effigy.
For when I saw her freshly fallen in the woods
I knew she was more than ancient tree.
But a Shining One, who, long ago to escape
the fate of iron and flame that raged over Albion,
stepped from this path and into the soft grain
of a seedling to seal herself safely within.
On the tail of that storm hung a phoneme,
on the lap of the Nidd it flowed again,
the drip of rain from the leaves above spoke
another guttural letter; when heard together
they said *Beag*, a word that will release her
from her sleep in the cell of sap and rings.

And now in the chamber the visitor whispers
the word I heard the woods and river say,
the word that floats in water, a name
to untie the knots, open doors and blur
all the edges. Ursula stirs and the sound
of bees rises with a mist that chills the room
despite the fire's roar. The visitors tremble,
some flee in a goose-flesh rush, some remain,
stare for an instant through the gates into fairy,
over stepping stones, across a river of blood,
to a quiet grim Field of the Fallen, at a maiden
who comes dancing from a barrow mound
between spread-eagled corpses of warrior kings
and whispers something just for the visitor's ears.


As quickly as it came the cold mist clears,
the vision disperses, the drone of bees recedes.
Only the crackling spit of fire fills the chamber,
and the visitors, shaken, give thanks to Ursula,
gather their belongings and head for home
towards a fate they think they know a little better
than before and surmise they can now control.
And I am left with a besom to sweep, clean the blade,
rinse the bowl, open the shutters to the stars and sky,
let fresh air brush the remnants of the smoky gates
away and guide my dog-tired bride to bed to dream,
and as she sleeps I lie awake once more, strung
across the early hours, riddled with things half seen
from the relative safety of the lattice screen.

# Part 2
# MDXXVIII

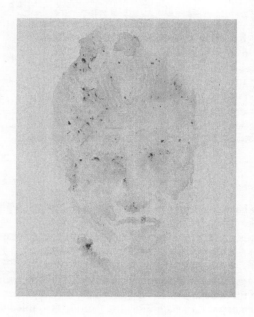

*'When the Cow doth ride the Bull,*
*Then, Priest, beware thy skull.'*

Mother Shipton

The visitors have increased and so has our fee,
and with it the ranking of those seeking answers.
How many truths have come to pass I cannot guess
and often ponder to what extent my wife has carved
the present design of life from beside the great log fire,
with her tongue turning fortunes like sweetmeats;
and if she did so even before we met; was it my
decision to wander the Long Walk after the storm
or did she call me through the howling wind
and drumming rain, did I feel myself that day?
Was I haunted by a nagging urge? I don't recall.
The years have passed and on and on the river flows,
the tales and drops of blood have filled her bowl
and I still lack the foresight to understand her goal.


Times have changed for England, a new chapter begins,
For The Royal Defender of The Faith is now estranged
from his maker; he who sided with Pope Leo against
Luther's army of dissenters now employs theology
to justify his carnal appetite for Anne Boleyn
and wrest some reason for the string of stillborn heirs.
While the Queen drowns herself in cloistered prayer
King Henry wakes each morning from his troubled dreams
of reaping excesses from the bloated jowls of religion.
Throughout the realm people muse that he has fallen
under Black Nan's enchantment and is bound to plunge
England whole into eternal flame just to quench
the fire that courses through his veins like poison.
Though few are those who'd dare speak this fortune.

Within the looking glass in which I shave
the years have begun to etch themselves
in creases, in receding hair, in the white flecks
of stubble, the girthing of my trunk,
the niggling aches - far from growing pains,
in the distance of eyes that have glimpsed
inside the hardened shell of other people's lives
as they poured out pleas they'd tell no other,
while I've eavesdropped on their audience.
But Ursula, no, she does not alter; in sixteen years
she's not aged with folds of skin, flaps, scars,
wrinkles, but is as when I carved her shape,
except for a certain smoothness, a light sheen of
elbow grease where my rough hands have held her.


I find October to be the loneliest month,
a month full of threadbare holes from which
omens emerge like russet words, a time
for choosing and withdrawing, approaching Samhain,
for letting go and for storing what will be needed.
When the woods turn hard and wet and begin
to open up its spaces -  new found distances stain
the traveler, who should take care to mind his step;
and, beyond the Fall, the waiting stillness
of encroaching frost creeping from the hollows.
Out of one such hole rides Sheriff Besley
with three cowled companions, as full of disdain
as an Autumn night has for sunlight; practiced
in the art of stubbing out an irksome life.

Besley announces their October names,
they shake my hand, and I know them at once
as the loyal chicks of the Metered Peacock.
Their firm hands have shed blood in France,
are accustomed to the sword, mace and lance
and the torch hurled into wattle and thatch;
hold no qualms of sliding a dagger into a back.
My maid, Anne, takes their coats and feathered hats.
Would they like bread and wine after their journey,
and from where had they travelled? 'London.'
They eat their fill, drink a pitcher of elder wine.
As their eyes rove about the room they speak
in low grumblings, of which all I hear with any
clarity is, 'So where resides this witch?'


As Anne prepares the chamber for the visitation
I keep the visitors occupied with light chat and wile.
They wear doublets of leather, velvet, heavy brocade,
two with the Spanishe Worke, in the slashed style,
decorated with the Royal coat of arms, jewels inlaid.
So I inquire of court fashion and of new dances,
and recount how the wild moors of North Yorkshire
are renowned as falconry land, and the forests
around Rievaulx perfect for hunting stag and boar,
or so it's said by those who know; yet they appear
unimpressed, so I mention just how rare it is for
courtly men of noble birth to pay a casual call on Ursula,
and may I be so bold to venture where they are bound?
'Heading toward Lord Clifford's estates in Cumberland.'

Their answers are curt, the growls of restless curs,
but shortly Anne slips in to announce with a curtsy
that Mistress Shipton is ready to see them now.
Would they like an audience one by one or as a group?
I take my leave while she explains the particulars
of paying, knocking, the greeting and being seated
at the table with the bowl of water, ink and blade.
I settle behind the screen while Ursula sits like stone.
Then comes the threefold knock, the door swings open,
one of them enters with a greeting of Good Health.
The fire crackles, a chair leg scrapes, the soft brush
of the atheme unsheathed, then a snort of contempt,
'Enough of this farce, what is this puppet show?
Shipton the Oracle is naught but a mannequin!'


This visitor barks, rising up from his chair,
'Carpenter I see you and what you are worth.'
He pulls back the screen, the knife in his fist
to see me cower in shadows, drags me out
with a handful of hair bellowing, 'You Sir would
make a fool of me and my King with this charade.'
The cold edge presses at my throat as I stammer,
'The seer before us is more than you would suppose.
Slit my throat as a charlatan by all means, Good Sir,
but first do as Anne advised, complete the ritual, only
then decide if this be naught but a fairground ride.'
He cuts his own palm flesh, blood falls to swirl.
Through the smoke comes the drone of angry bees.
The man looks at the witch and calls out, '*Beag.*'

The low murmur becomes a timbered voice,
*You are far from home Sir John Brydges,*
*have you ventured North by choice*
*or on account of one's secret pledges*
*to Ipse Rex – not the king himself?*
The visitor sinks uncomfortably into his seat,
eyeing the rows of veils and jars upon the shelf
above the stove, then, shaking despite the heat,
says, 'Mistress Shipton, if you, in truth hold
the power they claim, your Sight will see
who has purchased me with gifts of fool's gold.
If so, I ask if one day I shall wake to be free?'
Ursula replies *These chains will soon break.*
His time in The Tower would be for his own sake.


At this he flinches and grows embittered,
'This is a malign occupation in which you trade!
News has reached the Court of your littered
lies that threaten laws which ought to be obeyed.'
*Not so, Sir John,* she softly sighs, *I merely*
*answer questions to the counsel that is sought,*
*and lay before the seeker those spreading rings*
*of incidents perceived in the petrifying waters*
*of the future's dropping well. Behold before*
*your eyes within the water, blood and ink,*
*is that not you upon a battlefield facing*
*a Pilgrimage of Grace, your sword drawn*
*against Christ himself hanging on the cross,*
*and a chalice with a painted communion cake?*
'There are laws against quacks and fortune tellers',
he growls. The wood smiles, *Is that all you consider me?*
From his doublet he withdraws a scroll, 'I have papers!'
*The weightiest matters,* says she, *are oft dispatched*
*by a simple act, a mere signature, a seal stamped on wax*
*that binds a man to a destiny like a trout to a line.*
'That I know,' he replies, pained by his own taut fate.
*But the immediate act,* says Ursula, *rarely occurs*
*without a build up, without a flow, without some tremor*
*of warning, if only our eyes are keen enough to spot it.*
*And that be my business, Gentle Sir.* Brydges dabs
at his nose with a pomander stuffed with cloves.
'You are a threat to his Grace, a threat to his kingdom!'
*Some suspect a darker witch lies closer to his heart.*

He lays the unopened scroll upon the table,
'My master does request that you desist from
the spread of malicious gossip, treacherous fable,
this blasphemy you babble like love charms.
You would do far better, Lady or Golem
or Hedgewitch, to stick to weather predictions,
mixing up balms for sick cattle or to ease a rash.'
*Your master is a man of many talents, many titles,*
she replies, *Archbishop of York, Bishop of Lincoln,*
*Bishop of Tournai, Bishop of Durham, Cardinal,*
*Lord Chancellor, The Architect of Universal Peace,*
*as well as The Holy Wolf, The Butcher's Cur,*
*absent father, errant husband. Do we both not know*
*how he is as ravenous a snake as he is subtle?*
*I suggest you bide your time Sir Brydges*
*for you will outlive this snake, outlive the King,*
*outlive your secret love; the sad lady in grey.*
*Ride now from this shire to inform your master*
*that his time fast unfolds. Archbishop in name*
*he may well be, but never shall he walk*
*the cobbled shambles within the walls of York.*
Her voice cracks, splits, buzzes, flies from
one dim corner of the chamber to another,
any animation that had transfigured the grain
of the face vanishes as quick as it had come.
The fire crackles and the chair leg scrapes.
Sir John Brydges wipes his bearded lips
with a handkerchief of lace, bows, departs.

*Good day to you, Lord Darcy*, says my witch-wife
to our second visitor of the night, as he takes
the offered seat, saying 'Good Health,'
raises his cup then sips, 'though I suspect
you would be less hospitable if you understood
our purpose here, perhaps Sudley has been opaque?'
*Sudley has been as clear as day*, she hums.
'And what, Lady, do you see through me?' he enquires,
slicing a finger and squeezing out a large red berry.
*Take note, Thomas, of the patterns of chance,
see how you ride to ruin for the five glorious wounds,
how your head, once stolen, rolls all the way to France.*
'What!' he bellows, upturning the bowl of destiny,
'Mark this as surety, the Cardinal shall burn thee!'


The door bursts open as the third barges in,
sword already drawn, 'Darcy, what is amiss?',
he barks, striding close to Thomas' side.
'I'll cut out this witch's tongue,' he snarls.
'I swear the Cardinal will treat her as kindling,
thereafter her soul will perish in The Pit.'
*Only if this burns first*, cries Ursula, as her
scarf is tossed into the fire where it writhes
in flickering lights, spitting blues and greens
but resisting the kiss of even the hottest flames.
*I know my end, Charles Brandon. I'll show you
yours, as I did this Lord's, if you so wish it,
but I'll tell you this without a drop of humour,
I shall not burn for thee, nor for thy Peacock.*

# Part 3
# MDXXXVII

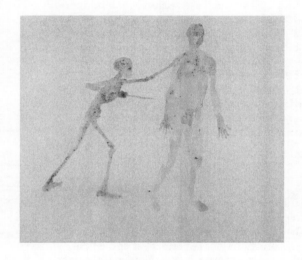

*'Jesu Christ and Saint Benedict*
*Bless this house from every wicked wight.'*

Chaucer, *The Miller's Tale*

On and always the Old Nidd comes and goes
under World's End Bridge, around stepping stones,
Spring flooding its banks, frozen in Winter,
carrying the litter of life away through the Dale,
to lose itself in the Ouse at Nun Monkton.
Old Nidd is impervious to the on-goings of folk
that dwell by its flow; not ignorant but indifferent
to the reflections we cast over its inevitability.
All the while it looks back at us, bemused by
our efforts to control our flows, to enforce
our wills upon the eddies of turmoil, and in
the last ten years we have all rough ridden
a time of such great change, as the age-old
ways, the buttresses of being are dismantled.


Ursula continues to foresee the shifting tides
while I have acted as nurse, interpreter,
as her arms and her legs, as the shield at her side,
as her protector, her concealer - if and when
and as the day demands. For some months
we returned to the cave in the woods by the well,
for a while we lodged with a Trinitarian Friar
in the Chapel of Saint Giles, while agents
of Cromwell sought Ursula; first as a heretic
like the Holy Maid of Kent, then as an item
of superstitious idolatry like a common market
cross or a painted figurine of the Virgin,
whose eyes will miraculously open at a pull
of a thread to weep tears of lamb's blood.

As we look up at the Plough from the cave mouth
I curse King Henry and the whole of his Tudor court.
She bids me bide my time, place my trust in the flow:
*All around the throne eventually fall under its thunder.*
*Was not Wolsey snared on a charge of Praemunire,*
*and flayed by his own abuses of ecclesiastical power*
*upon the blade of his failure to solve the 'Great Matter'?*
*Thomas Cromwell will find his fate little different,*
*even Cranmer will die from a fall from royal favour.*
'And Norfolk, what of Thomas Howard?' I press her,
for the Good Catholic and his troops had returned to create
bloody spectacles in the gardens of Yorkshire's villages
with the innards and quarters of so many pilgrims.
*He too will worm his way into a cell within the Tower.*


The holy commotion last October led
to many new visitors seeking reassurance
after Aske's call to arms, divining whether
they'd number among the survivors. Devout men
from hamlets and outlying farms, sons and fathers
used to a life tilling the ground, fed on diet of Mass
as on ravel, not villains to be bought off for a shilling,
but honest men of firm conviction who believe
in the Church's restoration, in a Northern parliament;
that to march, to fight and die is an obligatory
sacrifice to gain the King's acknowledgement,
to avert the realm's swift slide toward anarchy.
Resolute and fearful, and so were their wives,
cleaning off the rust and sharpening their knives.

The first to arrive at our home was Denys Bywater,
a Thirsk cobbler, who sat solemnly not daring
to look directly at Ursula, instead kept his eyes
locked on the fire to ask if there would be enough
with the heart and stomach to respond to Aske's call,
enough to make a point, to dent the armour
of the Privy Council, 'Enough to be heard by a King?'
In the bowl of swirling blood and ink he saw
an army of forty thousand marching men, singing
with a common grudge to the bridge over The Don
to shout down the token force led by The Duke.
Behind the horde lay York, already fallen,
before him all of the captains and counsellors
wrangling to pacify the ranks without bloodshed.


Charles Stainthorpe, a young tanner from Ripon,
asked Ursula Shipton if he would fall in battle,
would he return intact to marry his sweetheart?
*Only*, she'd said, if he slips away unseen
from the camp, from singing the battle anthem
on the heights of Scawsby,
                'In your hearts
                put away all fear and dread
                and take afore you the cross of Christ.'
and venture to the banks to water The Don
in the teeming rain, then return, so the river
shall swell in the night to cut off both forces;
*the imminent engagement must be averted*,
only then would he avoid the crushing fate
of his exposed skull meeting a whirling mace.

John Merryweather, a baker from Knaresborough,
arrived late one eve with his brother Richard.
Richard waited, fidgeting outside, as the elder
performed the ritual that brought the wood to life,
to help him to wrestle the split in his conscience.
'I am a loyal subject of His Grace, I am no traitor,
but our father raised us to follow the Good Lord.
I cannot bear the willful butchery of our faith
to justify the earthly wants of the pampered nobility.
He has stolen the First Fruits and cast us adrift,
but will this campaign lead us to do something
unspeakable to the sovereign?' *Watch your brother,
John Merryweather, for this be the Year of Judas.
Henry will remain unharmed to reap a red revenge.*


And others came to the house and later the cave:
Matthew Bigge, the Wetherby Blacksmith
pressed into service on the threat of his children's
slaughter, his forge and home looted and torched.
Edmund Foxgate, who walked from Cleveland
with a troop of hardy labourers, under the banner
of St Cuthbert, brimming with resentment
and eager for engagement with the Lord's enemy.
By the cliff he declared, 'For a man to die in defence
of Christ is nothing to fear, it will ensure his entry
into God's own kingdom, but what of the North?
Will we be remembered?' *Life and death are
the same, as river and tree are one*, she droned.
'Oracle, a red pox on all riddles!' spat Foxgate.

Turning to leave the gloom of the cave he glanced
from her to me with that questioning look
I'd observed before - a resentful river pike's
beneath the surface tension - what right had I
to squat on my haunches, lulled by the well's drip
when good men left their homes and their wives
to place their necks on the executioner's block?
*He who desires but acts not, breeds pestilence!*
But I knew the fear, I felt the calling and oft' woke
in a sudden sweat of cowardice, guilt's fingers
probing my chest, but in truth I could not bear
to leave her side, and suspect that most sense
this too and not judge too harshly my abstinence
from the march toward salvation, death and glory.


So off they trudged on their civil crusade
to rescue the true faith's prodigal son
from the snares His Grace had set himself,
and, as they vanished into the Autumn woods,
their anthem disturbing nesting crows, soliciting
a grating chorus of warning, I imagined
them charging full-tilt towards windmills,
stumbling headfirst into the season's holes.
Norfolk offered the rebel shepherds a pardon,
to all but ten, to avoid unchecked rebellion.
The Pilgrims refused and pressed hard for battle,
rattling their swords against their shields
on the hilltops like their Danish forebears,
striking at rain clouds with their billhooks.

So much of warfare is the endless waiting,
for those at the front and those left behind.
Measured on small talk around smouldering
camp fires, the sleepless hours through nights
of listening, days dilated as if on labour pains
while a father paces and wrings his hands
for the news of the birth of a healthy heir.
On the field this birth is the call to die,
hanging ever-expectant in the smoky air.
Now the families ventured to inquire of omens,
'Did my father fall at the siege of Scarborough?'
'Has my Charles learned to dodge the cannon?'
Then word arrived that the Crown had agreed
to listen to the grievances of Aske's delegation.


I'd watched those men leave in fearful determination,
Hope's fires flickering bright in their hands.
Now they drift back in triumph, though frozen
through snowflakes blanketing familiar lands,
clutching pardons, promises, hard won bargains,
some muttering, 'Pretium Laborum Non Vile'
(Not a bad reward for labour), and claiming
their efforts had all proved worthwhile. *But*,
warned Ursula, *His Grace is an adder, cold blooded,
fork-tongued, who minds it unnecessary to keep
His word; withdrawing what once was awarded,
including a pardon, and for the sake of his sleep
sends Norfolk back to cause such dreadful execution
in villages he has marked for a royal retribution.*

January too is a waiting time, all our ears
straining to keep abreast of the rumbling thunder
of bitter discontent across three Ridings
and from over the Pennines, fuelled by the bills
requesting assistance from all good neighbours
to muster on Richmond Moor. Sir Francis Bigod's
failed insurrection grants Henry enough reason
he hardly needs to repeal the pardons, to root out
any sign of unrest in his Northern gardens
and publicly wring its neck. We anticipate reprisals
worse than those following the Lincolnshire Risings.
A summons is issued for every wapentake
to give the oath before Norfolk's deputies,
to submit themselves to the mercy of the King.


Watching from the crowd today I witnessed
John Merryweather examined in an orderly fashion,
found guilty and asked if he was repentant,
if his actions had offended God and his Majesty.
John was pale, haggard, his eyes overstuffed
with the Winter's sky, standing on that platform
between masked guards, his words were pebbles
dropped into a pool of faces, 'I worthily deserve
this death. I beseech God's and all men's forgiveness.
Take example by me for committing the like.
And brother, I forgive thee.' He was stripped, hung,
cut down, kicking, his guts opened, innards drawn
and burned before his eyes, before being quartered
and suspended in the four corners of the square.

As his twitching body was opened, unfolded,
and the wooden platform swilled in his blood,
in the audience's gasps, roars of fascinated
revulsion and someone's uncontrollable giggles,
I tore my gaze away from the gruesome play
not wishing to see the world inside turned out,
and watched instead the steady drip of blood
seeping between the rough platform's boards
splash the frosty ground, the blades of grass,
the tight cluster of snowdrops by the wall,
resilient in the clutches of the two-faced god.
Each fine stalk, destitute of leaves, bearing
a single pendulous bell-shaped flower-head,
their three ghostly outer petals streaked red.


This oath of allegiance provides licence
for the unscrupulous to settle old feuds
by denouncing as traitors innocent folk
against whom they have long held grudges.
In their scouring for crime the deputies
arrive one crisp February morning, mounted
on geldings, at the mouth of St Robert's Cave
where we are holed up. 'Tobias Shipton!'
one calls, another dismounts and peers
into the darkness of our hovel. 'Show thyself!
I arrest you on the charge of treason.'
I strip Ursula of her garments, quickly
lay her in a corner and venture out to greet
their set glares, to be led away to gaol.

'And where is your wife?' asks the deputy.
'My wife?' I say, while one of his lackeys
binds my wrists with the end of a long cord.
'Aye, the woman known as Mother Shipton.'
'My wife left to visit Masham two days gone.'
He scans the woods, orders two of his men
to ride on to Masham, 'Find her and bring the witch
to York for trial'. He sends three off to scour the cave
and woods, 'Weed her out if she's hiding nearby.
Meanwhile we shall lead this one to the castle.
Take his boots.' He who'd tied my hands gives
the length to his master, who spurs his horse
to a walk, dragging me along in their wake.


In town people stop to watch our procession,
some I know well turn to look at the wall.
As we pass into the market place and the stalls
a crowd gathers on either side; whispers
flutter like wood pigeons' wings, among them
I hear my name repeated and 'Where's Ursula?'
'Where is Mother Shipton?' The deputy calls,
'Make Way! Stand back!' His horse snorts,
then I hear the buzz, smell and see, suspended
above my head, the blackened, severed left leg
of John Merryweather as we enter Castlegate.
The cord digging into the flesh of my wrists,
my feet torn and numb, I ask Death, beside me,
*Is she safe? Will they realise their mistake?*

I'm led limping down worn, stone steps, through
a heavy door into the clotted stink of the hold;
half a dozen men are penned there behind bars,
in a menagerie of misery, fear and sickness.
In the spluttering light of the single torch in the sconce
I see them regarding me with dark ringed eyes
that have had ample time to contemplate their fate.
I see in those rings the hours spent beseeching
The Lord, questioning, pleading, then riling against
the One they'd willingly taken up arms to defend,
His Kingdom on Earth, His holy days and shrines;
stood their ground against the might of the Crown
only to find themselves forsaken and broken.
My own faith has led me to the very same place.

# Part 4
## MDXXXVII

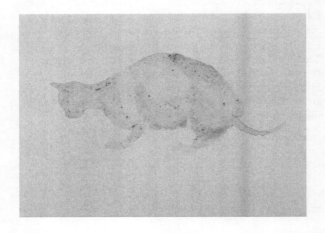

*'Like truthless dreams, so are my joys expir'd,*
*And past return are all my dandled days;*
*My love misled, and fancy quite retir'd*
*Of all which pass'd the sorrow only stays.'*

Sir Walter Raleigh

Left to stew in my own brew of hopelessness
hard upon the pallet, staring at the ceiling,
I hear a voice call from a gloomy recess,
'Tobias? Tobias Shipton. Toby, is that you?'
'I am naught but a dead man, friend and so are you!'
My own voice cracked, dry and brittle as chalk.
'Curb your tongue. They have yet to take your guts.'
the voice rebukes, 'We are to be tried in York
and much can happen between now and then.'
Something twigs, I raise myself for a closer look
and recognise the man as William Tymewell,
who I had known as a boy, had once gone out
hoggling with during the parish ale of Young Men.
He casts me a smile like a rope on which to cling.


Will informs me of my festering companions:
Thomas Staverley from Aysgarth who'd ridden
across the Ridings, rabble rouser and messenger;
Anthony Peacock, one time bailiff, now a collector
of offences like pearls on a string, from cattle theft
to sparking a riot and looting in Barnard Castle,
leading a body of rebels in Richmondshire's Risings;
Roger Hartlepool, a Jervaulx Cistercian who had
traded his white habit for a studded leather harness,
his hoe and his crook for a battle axe and buckler;
Edward Kytchen, who had marched in Lincolnshire
with Captain Cobbler and escaped the executions;
and the last of the six chained in the stronghold,
Richard Merryweather, the brother of poor John.

All of them rounded up, awaiting interrogation,
all bruised and bearing wounds from ill treatment.
All rats that left it too late to abandon a sinking ship.
All sharing their fugitive tales of flight, fight
and betrayal, some full of regret, eager to repent.
I tell Merryweather I had witnessed John's death,
heard his announcement of forgiveness to his brother.
Richard tells me they were fleeing toward Cumbria
when the militia picked up their scent in a Teesdale inn,
they'd slipped out at dawn into the snow-choked yard,
John was apprehended in the stables, attempting
to steal horses, while he had crouched, hidden
by a dry stone wall. 'But what could I do, but run,
keeping low, vanishing into the moorland's folds?'


Hartlepool recounts how too many men of high
condition are now wriggling like white maggots
from the corpse of a Trojan horse and fawning
all over the Duke in an attempt to improve
their standing. Ralph Ellerker and Robert Bowes,
even Aske himself, are busy making the rounds
as part of Norfolk's entourage, implicating others
from the rebel council, 'Their purpose ambition,
their practice only hate.' And the word is, Bigod
has been captured in Cumbria, John Hallam
executed in Hull, the Percy brothers summoned
to London, while Lord Darcy is on the run
somewhere in East Cleveland on a last ditch
effort to raise another force with Bulmer.

During our imprisonment sleep is fitful,
the dreams begin as they had on those nights
between finding my wife on the river bank
and returning to haul her back to my workshop,
all those years ago. Strange, troubled dreams:
starting with a lilting song as sweet as mead,
a flute of surf carried on the wordless breeze,
a sharp lament that sparks an aching hollowness
deep within, sets the heart skipping a beat,
hums through bones, then the visions come,
the slow red river, stepping stones, a black rock,
the grim barrow under a great sinking sun,
a field of slain kings, flapping banners in tatters,
a carpet of wild flowers, the air clothed in crows.


And here I stoop on the wrong river bank,
crying; 'Ursula, forgive me!
I have failed as Guardian of the Sacred Wood,
as surely as ever I always knew I would.
Though you must have known that too.

Ursula,
do not forsake me!
How many others have failed to protect you
throughout the long centuries,
those skeletal kings,
the children of Danu?

Now I know not where you lie,
what hands manhandle your distorted form,
which of our secrets have been untied.'

The velvet tune floods the mind's spare corners,
echoes around the cell until the old stones ring,
makes my shackles sing. And the vision shifts to
a barren land where the dead march and run amok
herding the living, wailing, through shallow trenches
into a tunnel beneath a hill. A sumptuous feast
is scattered and trodden by fleshless feet, coffins
belch from freshly dug graves to spill their cold
contents who go shambling after life, starting fires,
collecting heads, ringing bells; there is nowhere
to run nor hide, smoke darkens the sky and someone
somewhere strums upon a lute, keeping his tunnelled
gaze glued upon his lover's to block out the horror.
But in this hell even babes and kings fall victim.


I wake in a sweat with a start or scream and ask
my caged companions, 'Can you not hear the din?
Can you not hear her calling?' Yet they cannot
and look upon me as one as if I were a prize fool.
But the song was there, clear as the spluttering torch,
the vision as real as the thresh of mildewed straw.
I am shaken by lingering images, the pounding
of the Reaper's drums, the familiar faces of the dead,
while the distinctions between us and them dissolve.
What if all our efforts in this doomed revolt
spring from the ageless fear to face a new future,
the blind refusal to adjust to new philosophies,
to ways only so recently considered heretical?

'If it's a song you need to calm your nerves,
to clear your mind', calls William Tymewell,
'then find some strength in this...' and begins
to croak in a voice like grinding corn,
      'Christ crucifyed!
      For they woundes wide
      Us commens guyde!
      Which pilgremes be
      Through godes grace,
      For to purchase
      Olde welth and peax
      Of the spiritualtie.'
One by one the rest take up the tumbled tune
until we all sing together, rattling our chains.


Me and William high kicking through leaf piles,
out hoggling on an owl's hoot for the parish ale
of Young Men and stalking settling shadows,
talking Robin of the Hood, fencing with sticks,
purses full of small coins and browned conkers.
From out of the alley onto Kirkgate, just ahead,
stepped Agnes Rose Stokesley, making to hurry,
a long cloak hanging from her shoulders, lips pink
as cherry blossom, a wicker basket on her arm.
We stopped to watch the shape and swing of her,
the stretch, shrink, growth of her sliding shadow.
Saw her glance back as she slipped into church.
We waited past the bells, wondering what lay in
her basket; why such a late visit to Father Barnard?

'And what mischief are you two boys about?'
Agnes Rose asked when she finally appeared.
'Please permit us to escort you on your route,
out of concern for your welfare,' volunteered
William, offering his arm like a gallant courtier
and sending Agnes into a bubbling fit of giggles.
'Do you often visit the priest following Vespers?'
'The poor man gets lonely during his long vigils.'
'I thought that,' I said, 'was the point to Nocturnes.'
'The point,' teased Agnes 'is what you make it.'
Handing me her basket she and William turned
in the shade of the wall. The contents concealed
by a cloth I wouldn't remove. Then Will held
the basket as I lost my first delights with Agnes.


The following morning our stronghold door
is unlocked by a keeper who enters ahead
of a visitor wrapped in a woven shawl.
Outside we catch a flash of fallen snow
then the guard slams the door and waits
while the woman comes close to the bars
and peering through the gloom mutters,
'Mr Shipton, are you alive? Come nearer.
It is I, Anne, Anne Cooke your housemaid.'
I ask her why she has come, 'It is not safe!'
She says she has suffered from a plague
of bad dreams, the smell of burnt wood.
I beg her for news of Ursula. She had none.
'Then seek the Friar, implore him to find her.'

Some hours later our cages are unlocked,
we're loaded in our shackles onto a cart.
Under guard we set off from the castle,
winding through the white shrouded town,
shivering in a biting wind we huddle close.
'We are bound for York' says Tymewell.
'Where we shall face examination and trial'
adds Hartlepool. 'Fear not,' murmurs Peacock,
'All is arranged. We shall be rescued on the way
by a loyal band from Swaledale.' So we watch
the trees, the Vale's rolling fields, past churches
stripped of images, their lights extinguished,
but by the time we reach Providence Green
even Peacock has given up hope of any rescue.

# Part 5
# MDXXXVIII

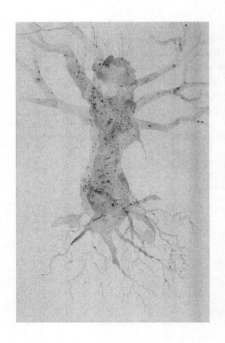

*'A fire. A fire is burning!*
*I hear the boot of Lucifer*
*I see his filthy face!*
*And it is my face and yours,'*

Arthur Miller, *The Crucible*

York dungeon is such an infernal hole
of finely calculated cruelty, that upon our first
entering I knew my hellish vision had come
to pass and found a perfect home from home
in this pit of footsteps, drips and shrieks,
clanging doors and rattling keys, where
the darkest wanderings of enquiring minds
become manifest, and the human body
and eternal spirit are put to inhuman tests,
against devices spawned from fevered incubus;
What makes up a renaissance man?
What will break him swiftly or slowly?
What will turn him into an animal, vegetable
Or a quivering river of pouring liquid?


Time itself has the sharpest barb, it hooks
and twists and hoist you up on high, dangling
the stretched frame on a weighted strappado
in preparation for its public display, once
the spark of life has fled the broken husk.
I have learned to close my ears to all but echoes
of my pulse, stopped my mind from registering
what my eyes settle upon and give myself
over to a nothingness carried on the breath.
But these meditations cannot last all day
or night and rumours pass on soft bat wings.
The King's Examiner has arrived in the city,
it is said he has a keen taste for blood.
His name a mere whisper, John ap Rice.

Some say he is a demon loosed from hell
dressed in a coat of human skin, one
who needs never shout but whose speech
is a soft caress that leaves a nasty sting,
a patient man, list maker, wheedler, lie detector
adept at extracting the desired answer, a man
with Baphomet reclining in each pupil,
who will sup on shrieks and chew the groans
of each anointment in the rites of torment.
A man with royal licence to use all the means
he can devise by all kinds of tortures and
otherwise to enforce the suspect to declare
the whole and plain truth of all things.
Steeling myself I await his summons.


Three times did I meet John ap Rice;
a short, thick badger of a man with darksome,
underground eyes, broad hands, stubby digits
with finely manicured nails, a well trimmed
russet beard, which, as he spoke, he would gently
stroke like a familiar with his index finger
from his nose downward, across his lips
to trace the coarse shape of his cleft chin.
I saw no wild demon dancing in his gaze;
this man was all formality, calculated yet
courteous, with a clearly set duty to perform.
I feared John ap Rice was all too human.
At either side sat Mr Tregonwell and Mr Legh,
bound to assist him in the King's enquiries.

For the first examination they sit at a table,
each with papers arranged, quills and ink pots.
I am strapped into the stretching chair
by the hands of another, who I do not see
but under John's direction feel his work acutely.
Click
Rice confirms my name, age and place of birth,
then enquires, 'Had I wed one Ursula Sontheil
now known as a witch and as a prophetess?'
I answer, '*Yes, I am Ursula's husband*', and Legh
and Tregonwell scribble notes on parchment.
Click
John ap Rice asks, 'Where has your wife fled?
Do you admit to committing treason in word or deed?
What do you know of Peacock, Merryweather,
Tymewell, Staverley and Edmund Kitchyn?
Can you confirm the Cistercian is Roger Hartlepool?
Are you acquainted with a Friar called Robert Esch?'
Click
'Who devised the letters sent to stir the country
and those pinned up on the parish church doors?
Who was responsible for distributing copies
of the outlawed Mouldwarp Prophesy?
What have you heard of the new teaching and the old
and what complaints and from whom did they come?'
Click
'Who were the ringleaders of the Richmond Commotions,
the Barnard Castle Riots, and in the treasonous
insurrections against their most loyal Sovereign?'
Click
'What are your opinions on the matter of Supremacy?
What is your belief concerning Purgatory?
What names do you know of the women
who sallied forth at night to cut down
their husband's bodies from the Crown's gibbets
to bury them unlawfully in consecrated ground?'
Click
'Are you guilty of the crime of carving sacred images
for the purposes of idolatry? How deep
is your involvement in attempting to establish
an heretical cult around the worship of such an icon?
When was the last time you crept up to the Cross?'

Click
'Have you participated in a Black Fast against King Henry?
What do you know of the ritual baptism of a cockerel?
Do you keep three bees under a stone to call them forth
one by one by name and feed them with drops of blood?
What do you know of the manufacture of flying ointment
made chiefly from the fat of boiled children?'
Click
Click Click

Throughout the interrogation pain becomes a presence,
a physical being that prances around the chamber,
feeding on my grunts and groans and on the flat line
of question after question, on the sweat and the silence
of my torturer, 'til this Thing plucks Rice's voice
like a lute, and in my blistered sight wears the masks
of Mr Tregonwell and Mr Leigh, their quill hands
rising and falling on strings held between its beak,
and I feel its dark feathered wings stroke the foetid air
fanning the candle flames and the flame of my pain
rising, unfurling, petal upon petal, to engulf me
within a cloud of noble vapours, contaminating
my nostrils. This Thing begins to sing, *Tabun, Soman,
Sarin, Rycin,* ' til on wing beats I'm carried away.

Who can blame those who confess under pressure?
Who, amid the screams, incriminate the innocent,
just to secure a moment's respite, for you know
not what babble drools from between cracked lips
that writhe and sing of their own accord to the quiet
delight of the examiners' tide of questions,
each one a wave that leaves you drowning
amid the stutter of a murmured refrain.
*Dues in adiutorium meum intende*
*Dues in adiutorium meum intende*
*Dues in adiutorium meum intende*
'O God, incline unto my aid!' Knowing thyself naught
but a number and a note in a draft of a bishop's book
that travails to purge the realm by uniform discipline.


Some rumours rat-skitter through the corridors,
appear under locked doors like cockroaches;
some slide, leaving criss-crosses, swirls, spirals
of silver trails in the dark, while others weave
like a dusty ghost moth landing on the brickwork
of my scratching wall of boils and weeping sores
to preen its antennae; then off, back through gaps
between bars, past guttering torches to find a route
into the early Springtime air, leaving an inkling
of news, droppings of gossip. That's how word
gets around in prison; occurrences are known
without the memory of having been told - something
about the execution of Anthony Peacock that morning,
the real Hartlepool has crossed the border to Scotland,
a great many false icons of worship fuelled
a bonfire last night at the foot of Clifford's Tower,
the King's new Queen is expectant with child.

Prison is the vat in which to distil despair.
Mind and memory are unloosed to wander
vagrant days that pour out of blind spots:
I toss pebbles into Old Nidd from the middle
of World's End Bridge, my father guides
my saw hand through a plank of smooth oak.
I am twelve, watching Mother as she cooks
heavy and ripe with my brother or sister.
I watch her crumple in a groan to the floor,
spilt broth and blood mix together in a pool.
I am running, screaming, into the workshop.
I am watching my father roaring at the rafters.
He is holding her tight and stroking her face.
I watch October turn him, day by day, to stone.


My second summons came once I got wind
that Staverley had given up the ghost
in his cell after a stint of severe questioning.
I'd woken to guards dragging something limp
along the corridor. In the examination room
once more I am strapped to the chair facing
John ap Rice, Mr Legh and Mr Tregonwell
and brace myself for the flood of accusations.
It comes like a litany, many of the same,
though many more concerned Roger Hartlepool;
had I known him before being imprisoned?
What was his role in the October insurrection,
in the bill posting and the post-pardon riots,
which Abbots had he pressed into the rebellion?

Strange how my cell's darkest corner becomes
a haven in which to curl up my soft body
like a snail in a shell and try to smother the fire
Rice's man has kindled, using my bones as twigs
my flesh as a fan with which to tease the spark
to catch and spread through veins and ligaments.
I try to douse it in a stream of moans and shudders.
Staverley had died under such treatment and now
I begin to suspect that I will follow his lead,
be dragged limp into the light to be tossed in a pit.
Or was that just the easy option, far simpler than
facing the panel's harsh examinations again?
I call for the guard to request the materials
to make a full confession in my own hand.


Squatting in the shell-like dark with parchment,
ink pot, quill and my cup of drinking water,
thumb in my mouth I bite deep into the pad,
tear at the skin until I taste iron, feel its flow,
then drip a bulbous tear of ink into my cup
followed by a bright red plop, watch the colours
begin to spread and swirl and speak over the rim
the waking name, *Beag*, adding, *come to my aid!*
Within seconds comes the drone, the hollowness
growing as if my form were an egg being blown.
The marks on my scratching wall run and weave,
tunnel vision pulls like a hood about my head,
the drone becomes a roar and at the tunnel's end
the red river, the ragged banners and the mound.

I crouch on the bank beneath the flaming sky,
the black rocks of the stepping stones
disturbing the flow of the dark red current
roaring by, each one a scorched skull,
just too far apart to comfortably reach
but the song in the air tugs at my feet, so
I leap and land, not as a sack of raw bones
but with feline balance and upon all fours,
haunches coiled ready for the next launch
then out over the spitting fume and froth
that surges around each precarious rock,
until one leap takes me to the farthest bank
and I run, belly low, between the banners
darting into the waiting mouth of the barrow.


Then I am picking a path through the darkness
of an alley inside the city, ears pricked, padding
lightly, whiskers brushing the prison wall, nose
trained upon his scent leading like a winding
track to wherever he is lodged; with night
pressed close against my coat, on the balls
of my slit dilated eyes, alive to the tremors of air.
All around me come distractions: a warning
rustle, the rich smell of small prey and the sudden
savage thirst of raging instinct filling my throat;
a primordial purr threatening to drive off all other
impulses, any remnant of thought, all memory
of John ap Rice; but behind it the drone - within
it the seer song that will keep my tail in check.

Slink. Pause. Wait. Watch. Creep. Listen. Twitch.
Spring. Land. Settle. Dart. Twist. Huddle. Sniff.
Stalk. Pounce. Claw. Climb. Scrape. Trot. Sit.
Wait. Watch. Wait. Measure. Crouch. Shuffle.
Sail. Glide. Stretch. Reach. Lurch. Scramble. Skitter.
Cling. Slip. Fail. Fall. Slight. Slide. Roll. Right.
Bounce. Alight. Cower. Lurk. Loiter. Watch. Listen.
Wait. Sneak. Slither. Squeeze. Snake. Dash. Pad. Prowl.
Wriggle. Writhe. Edge. Inch. Tread. Steal. Flit. Weave.
Skirt. Cruise. Coast. Cringe. Flinch. Wait. Watch.
Wait. Stay. Strain. Shy. Shirk. Sidle. Scent. Shun.
Mark. Stain. Shake. Risk. Gain. Fence. Hedge. Feign.
Dodge. Race. Leap. Hurtle. Cross. Rise. Mount. Bound.
Approach. Wait. Squirm. Breach. Wait. Enter. Find.


His snores billow the plush bedchamber,
smells of wine, chicken, a stubbed out candle.
I cross the soft pile of the imported carpet,
spring lightly onto the feathered mattress
of the blanket-covered, four poster bed, then
step by step inch upward to sit upon his chest.
He shifts, his snores cease as my weight
affects his breathing, I lean closer, my whiskers
almost on his russet beard, his bed breath thick
upon my face, and then his eyes begin to flutter.
Half opening, glazed like a new born babe's
before the flood that comes with focus.
A long croak crawls out from between his lips
though he is unable to move his limbs or torso.

And so we watch and breathe deep of each other,
his gaze a green pool into which I lower a paw
to loosen the ties of all the ghouls he's secured
from thought in cages bound by duty and law,
disturbing the still surface of his loyal exterior.
I awaken him to himself. Sweat collects, spit drools
along his quivering cheeks to dampen his pillow,
until he sees with eyes that can no longer hide
the pleasures he draws from his work with pain.
His muscles spasm for every victim who cried,
each whimper a white hot brand searing his brain.
When I leap from his chest and flee like a shade
through the doorway, down the stairwell and out
into the night, I leave behind a very different man.

Two days hence I am handed a signed pardon,
led from my cell and released from prison.
I step slowly beside the sluggish Ouse,
watch seagulls glide about the dipping masts,
the sun bright on billowing sails, wander
as a vagrant shade, resting often, through
jostling streets to the market place; amongst
the calls of traders, the smells of produce:
meats, breads, leathers, beers, cheeses; children
playing sticks and pebbles, a length of worn rope,
dogs snap-fighting over scraps, billygoats
tethered to posts beside cages of chickens,
the cock-gentry's stroll through the cluck in colours
past unlanded peasants and commons
with cart wheels trundling, the tinkle of livery,
horse snorts, greetings, gossip, haggling,
coinage flashing, the peal of the Minster's bells.
I soak it all up like a salve to soothe my bones.
Drinking this pageant through every pore
as if it would fade in an instant, evaporate
and I would wake again in the cold, dark gaol.
Once, pausing, beneath the decaying remains
of Sir Robert Aske in chains I marvel how
the city goes on with its business, as always.
Meandering, I watch for a sign of any tail,
and as dusk falls cut deep into the shambles,
give the knock upon the door of the safe house
in Whip Ma Whop Ma Gate. A grille opens,
I say the word that will grant me entry.
Once within I know I'm safe, at least for a time.

The weeks following my release I have spent
recuperating in familiar hands, Anne Cook tending
to my comforts and my sores, and I have plagued
her with questions, to most of which she has replied,
'I do not know, wait, rest. Answers will come.'
I asked about Ursula's whereabouts, whether
she had heard anything, but she shook her head,
'Nothing more than rumours.' But earlier tonight
I was called down to the cellar to attend a meeting
of brothers. I recognised some faces of the eleven
who sat in a circle of chairs, including Esch and
Foxgate, all of them survivors of the King's wrath.
For an hour I was questioned on my incarceration,
the interrogations, why I had received a pardon.


I have nowhere and naught to hide so I tell
the truth of my memory of a feral cat's journey,
whether it be the hard fact itself or hallucination.
Then I ask of my wife, if she had been recovered.
If she had been destroyed, surely then my prison-
spell would have failed. 'Tobias', says Esch,
'First we must consider what you have told us
before we are able to provide you with answers.'
I hold no rage nor strength with which to refuse.
Anne escorts me back up the staircase where
I sit waiting beside the shuttered window,
listening to the rain drumming on the roof tiles,
the muffled tones of their muted conversation
creeping through the timbers of the house.

I must have drifted into a doze, for I started,
awake to find Anne stroking my shoulder,
a residual image staining my sight; the King
knelt in private prayer, bargaining with Christ,
granting anything in return for a male heir.
'Come Tobias,' says Anne, 'They give consent.'
Stiff and still in pain I follow her candle back
down the stairwell into the now silent cellar.
She settles upon one of the chairs arranged
in the circle, but at the centre as still as stone
sits Ursula Shipton, firelight dancing over
those heavy curves, the hard polished grain.
I fall down upon my knees, place my brow
upon the floor and, weeping, creep to her feet.

# Epilogue
## MDLXI

*'Here lies she who never lied,*
*Whose skill so often has been tried,*
*Her prophecies shall still survive*
*And ever keep her name alive.'*

Inscription upon Mother Shipton's
lost commemorative stone.

During the months of my incarceration
Ursula had been secreted by the band
of Esch's brothers, in a rough wooden coffin,
from cave to cellar, from priest hole to wagon,
to a relay of cobles running from Scarborough
to Whitby, Mulgrave, Steers, Skengrave, Coatham
and on to the old harbour town of Hartlepoyle,
where renegade Franciscans stored her safe
in the warren of smuggler's tunnels that riddle
the headland; while Norfolk's deputies scoured
the countryside for clues and John ap Rice's spies
ransacked homes and questioned the commons
for titbits of information that sent them chasing
will-o'-the-wisps down blind cuts and cul de sacs.


We lived through Edward's raging reforms,
the backlash of Queen Mary's red rule
and these long years with the Maiden Queen.
We did not return to Knaresborough but settled
in York, and frequently met the Brethren
who upon occasion brought us clients,
though they are few these days compared
to the flow that once sought her counsel.
Any wishing such a consultation must first
come through secret introduction followed
by thorough examination by the brothers.
Largely, I returned to carpentry, to working
with the good wood and fashioning furniture,
cabinets, clock cases in the new English style.

Six years before Edward became the Boy King
one determined man sought such an audience.
Arriving late at night with a single servant
he addressed as Will, who introduced his master
as a textile merchant. A bear of a man,
heavy with years who walked with a limp,
claiming they had travelled sorely from France.
Once more I lurked behind the screen as he
performed the ritual that woke the wood.
*You have made a long and unlawful pilgrimage,*
*my Lord. What is it you seek from me?*
'Answers.' This one was taciturn indeed.
*On what you cannot otherwise gain true counsel*
*because these are questions you dare not speak?*


From this man's heart swung a chain of thwarted dreams,
blood smeared upon a cloth of gold, so much bitter rage.
'My son...My legacy..,' a stammer swallowed.
He grimaced as he shifted his weight. 'Tell me, Crone,
if you are what I've heard, what does this future hold?'
*You are a poet, a musician, a warrior, a statesman*
*a lover, a monster, and your own worst traitor.*
'I know what I have been! I ask what is to come.'
*Your future is now.* She droned, *Your son will inherit,*
*though he shall meet the earth before he reaches manhood,*
*your daughter will dig up your remains and burn them.*
He sat for a time, staring heavy headed into the bowl;
when he looked up I saw his eyes were already dead.
Without another word the sad merchant and servant left.

Occasionally The Crown's commissioners have come,
scouring the realm for forbidden icons, vestments,
any remnants of the Old Faith; with increasing vigilance
since The Rising of the North and its quick suppression,
when Elizabeth proved she could reap a vengeance
even greater than her father's in his prime.

There has been a rise in witchcraft trials; people think
the Devil himself stalks at midnight plucking the innocent
from their paths to do his bidding, enslaved within a coven.

I have grown old and weary of the secret life.
Ursula still spouts her dream visions in bed beside me,
though I have learned now to sleep.

Whenever I do, I dream of a cat's wired nerves, a dry tongue,
a face full of smell and twitch and thirst and purr; that still
prowls around the dark shambles of my reposing thoughts.

But a new age is here, one of cold bright reason.
She tells me that an alchemist, a modern man
of scientific method, will be born this year;
time for the Faye to retreat further from sight.
We have made up our minds to follow the path
to the barrow, so upon the morrow I'll load Ursula
into my cart and we shall ride to Knaresborough;
trundle along the Long Walk and stop
by the Dropping Well. There I will take her, wrapped
in a shroud, and carry her to the water's edge.
I will kiss my wife, my Galatea, one final time
before easing her gently into the cold embrace,
weighting her down with rocks to make sure she sinks,
though not to drown but over time become stone.
Once my duty has been fulfilled, I will walk
the path by the river to where I first found her,
growing Hen of the Woods, a toad on her shoulder,
then wade into Old Nidd and let it take me
wherever it will, for it knows the flow so well.
It shall wash the years from my bones in its bed;
erase the aches and scars of the past, present, future
tense, release my spirit from this corporeal spool
and carry it cleansed to the surging sea of souls.

# Notes

Thanks are due to Crista Ermiya, editor of *Dogstar* in which some of these poems first appeared. Thanks also to Peter Hesleton for use of 'Division Well' for the cover image, to Andy Broderick for the images running through the book, to Kev Howard for the author photograph, and to Gordon Hodgeon for his keen eye and advice.

p12 The Dropping Well (aka The Petrifying Well). A natural well beside the River Nidd near Knaresborough, claimed to be England's first tourist attraction with visitors recorded from 1538. The water's extremely high mineral content means that everything in its path is turned into stone

p13 In Ovid's narrative, Pygmalion is a sculptor who carves a woman out of ivory. After seeing the real women of the city prostituting themselves, he loses interest in women, but his statue is so realistic that he falls in love with it. He offers the statue presents, names it Galatea and eventually prays to Venus, who takes pity on him and brings the statue to life.

p13 The River Nidd is a tributary of the River Ouse, rising in Nidderdale. The river then passes to the North of Harrogate before flowing through Knaresborough.

p13 During medieval witch-hunting, the term *maleficia* implied a pact with the Devil, and was used to describe any malicious acts by supposed witches or sorcerers.

p14 *Molochia* is the evil eye.

p16 Beag is the name of one of the Tuatha De Danann (Children of Danu) of Irish legend, a goddess who possessed a magical well of wisdom.

p22 The Metered Peacock is Cardinal Wolsey

p24 It is generally supposed that the three lords were the Duke of Suffolk, Lord Percy and Lord Darcy; however, as I was present I know that Wolsey was in fact represented by Charles Brandon the Duke of Suffolk, Lord Darcy and Sir John Brydges, the Baron Chandos of Sudley.

p29 Praemunire is the offence of appealing to or obeying a foreign court or authority, thus challenging the supremacy of the Crown.

p43 One of the pilgrim ballads of the Pilgrimage of Grace.

p64 Sir Francis Bacon (1561-1626), Renaissance author, courtier, and father of inductive reasoning.

p64 Once I had submerged Ursula in the well and said a prayer, I did indeed wade into the river and let it take me in its flow. However, I came to in a bed of a croft several miles down stream having been fished from the water like Moses and Taliesin. The fact that I have not been granted the peace of death for well over four hundred years is a matter explored in my other diaries.

## Further Reading

*Calendar of State Papers: Foreign & Domestic,* Vols 1536, 1537, 1538

Eamon Duffy, *The Voices of Morebath* (Yale, 2001)

Russell Hope Robbins, *Encyclopaedia of Witchcraft and Demonology* (Spring Books, 1967)

Arnold Kellet, *Mother Shipton: Witch & Prophetess* (George Mann Books, 2002)

David Loades (ed), *Chronicles of The Tudor Kings* (Garamond, 1990)

Geoffrey Moorhouse. *The Pilgrimage of Grace*, (Phoenix, 2002)